Grammar Book

Virginia Marconi

Contents

Was your vacation fun?

1 **Read the dialog. Where did Lucia and Pedro spend their vacations?**

Lucia: Hi, Pedro! Good to see you!

Pedro: Hi! Good to see you, too! I didn't see you this summer. Where were you?

Lucia: My brothers and I spent the summer on the coast, at my grandparents' vacation home.

Pedro: Was it fun?

Lucia: It was great! We went to the beach every day and we made a lot of friends. Grandpa has a boat so he took us fishing. What about you? Did you go anywhere?

Pedro: I went to a summer camp in July.

Lucia: How was it?

Pedro: It was great! My friend Carlos was there, too.

Lucia: What did you do?

Pedro: Well, we played all kinds of sports. We played soccer and volleyball. We went horseback riding in the mountains and canoeing in the river. We learned to play water polo, too.

Lucia: That sounds like fun!

Pedro: Oh, it was! Unfortunately, the summer camp was too short! The rest of the summer wasn't so much fun. My parents wanted me to review math for school. You know I'm not very good at math. So I had to do some review work every day.

Lucia: Oh, no! Poor you!

2 **Read and circle T (*true*) or F (*false*).**

1	Carlos is Lucia's friend.	T / F
2	Lucia's grandpa took her and her brothers fishing.	T / F
3	Pedro didn't enjoy the summer camp.	T / F
4	Lucia spent the summer by the ocean.	T / F
5	Pedro thinks the summer camp was too short.	T / F

Grammar

We **were** at my grandparents' house.	We **weren't** at school.
Was your vacation fun?	Yes, it **was**./No, it **wasn't**.
He/She/It **played** with a ball.	He/She/It **didn't play** with a ball.
We/You/They **went** to summer camp.	We/You/They **didn't go** to the beach.
Did you **enjoy** life at the camp?	Yes, I **did**./No, I **didn't**.

3 Read the dialog again and underline verbs in Past Simple.

4 Circle the correct answer.

My parents (wanted) / *wants me to learn to ride a horse last summer.*

1 Lucia's vacation home *weren't / wasn't* very big.

2 *Were / Was* your friends happy to go horseback riding on the hills?

3 My friends and I *didn't enjoy / did enjoyed* getting up early at summer camp.

4 I *went / didn't went* skateboarding at the camp.

5 What *were / did* you do at summer camp?

5 How are the verbs in sentence one and sentence two different? Discuss with a friend.

1 What did you enjoy at summer camp? I enjoyed canoeing in the river.

2 What film did you see last night? I saw a great thriller.

6 Write five questions using the phrases below. Then answer them for yourself.

play soccer/last week   Did you play soccer last week? No, I didn't.

●	1	ride a bike to school/last Saturday
	2	have lunch with your family/this weekend
●	3	go to the beach with your friends/last summer
	4	get up early/last Sunday
●	5	meet your friends at the mall/yesterday

7 Find a friend and take turns asking and answering your questions from Activity 6.

Did you play soccer last week?

Yes, I did. I played with Gustavo on Monday. Did you...

8  **Read what Susan wrote on her blog. Choose the best word (A, B, or C) for each space.**

This summer I had the best vacation ever! I _B_ to a summer camp in Devon. It **(1)** .... fantastic!

At the beginning, I was a little nervous, because I **(2)** .... know anybody. But after I **(3)** .... friends with Zoe, a girl from Canada, things changed.

What did we **(4)** ....? Well, our Group Leader **(5)** .... us up at 7 o'clock. Then, we **(6)** .... breakfast. After that, we **(7)** .... ready to begin our day!

There were so many things to do! We went mountain biking, canoeing, horseback riding, and since we were very close to the beach, we also went surfing... when the weather was good! ☺ I didn't **(8)** .... to come back!

So remember: next summer go to a summer camp! It's the best way to spend your vacation!

	A go	(B) went	C going
1	A is	B were	C was
2	A didn't	B don't	C did
3	A made	B make	C makes
4	A did	B does	C do
5	A made	B wake	C woke
6	A having	B had	C have
7	A was	B are	C were
8	A wanted	B wants	C want

The bus driver was running after the bus

1 Read the story. How did Robert become a hero?

A ten-year-old hero

Ten-year-old Robert Maxwell became a hero this morning when the seventh graders from Cedar Pines Elementary School were going on a school trip.

The children were talking happily when the bus driver decided to stop at a gas station to fill up. Apparently, he forgot to put the brake on the bus and it started rolling slowly down the hill.

The gas station manager called the police and the firefighters immediately. The bus driver was running after the bus when he saw it crash into a tree.

When he finally caught up with it, he saw Robert at the wheel.

"I was talking with my friends when I realized the bus was rolling down the hill," said Robert. "Dad taught me to steer a car, but he didn't teach me how to start or stop it. That's why I drove the bus into a tree."

When the police and the firefighters arrived, Robert's friends were taking photos with their hero.

2 Read and write *Yes* or *No*.

1   Robert was talking with his friends when he realized the bus was moving. ....

2   The gas station manager called the children's parents immediately. ....

3   The bus was going up the hill. ....

4   The bus driver stopped at the gas station because he wanted to fill up. ....

5   Robert drove the bus into a tree because he didn't know how to stop it. ....

3 Read the text again. Underline verbs in Past Progressive (*was*/*were* + verb + *-ing*) and Past Simple. Then fill in the table.

Grammar

The children **were talking** when the driver **decided** to stop the bus.

The bus .... going down the hill because the driver **forgot** to put the brake on.

When the police ...., Robert's friends **were taking** photos with him.

4 Circle the correct answer.

Last week, my mom and I walked with my dog Akira to the grocery store. We leashed her outside the store. When Mom and I ~~(were going)~~ / *was going* inside, Akira looked sad. We tried to be quick while we **(1)** *were shopping / were shopped.* When we **(2)** *were coming / were came* out of the store we **(3)** *saw / were seeing* that Akira

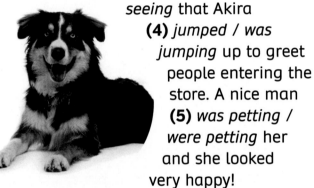

(4) *jumped / was jumping* up to greet people entering the store. A nice man **(5)** *was petting / were petting* her and she looked very happy!

5 Read the sentences and answer the questions.

1 The bus driver stopped at the gas station and forgot to put the brake on the bus.

2 I was talking with my friends when I realized the bus was rolling down the hill.

A Which sentence shows two completed actions?

B Which sentence shows that there was a long action in progress when something happened?

6 Last night after dinner, a thief climbed through the garage window to get into Skye's house. What was her family doing when this happened? Complete the sentences.

When the thief climbed through the garage window to get into Skye's home, she ___*was doing*___ (do) her homework in her bedroom. Her sister **(1)** _____ (watch) TV in the living room. Her brothers **(2)** _____ (play) computer games in their bedroom. Skye's dad **(3)** _____ (talk) on the phone in the kitchen and her mom **(4)** _____ (read) a book in the living room. The cats **(5)** _____ (sleep) under the window.

7 Now, write a continuation of the story. Use the phrases in the box to help you.

~~get~~ trip not see make noise
hear call the police arrive try
catch climb fall run away
put things in a bag

When the thief got through the window, he _____

_____

_____

_____

_____

_____

_____

8 Aarav is talking to his friend, Pierre, about his dad. What does Aarav say to Pierre?

Read the dialog and choose the best answer. Write a letter (A–H) for each answer. You do not need to use all the letters.

Pierre: Is your dad really a pilot?
Aarav: D

1 **Pierre:** Where did he fly yesterday?
Aarav: ....

2 **Pierre:** What time did he leave home?
Aarav: ....

3 **Pierre:** How did he get to the airport?
Aarav: ....

4 **Pierre:** What were you doing when he arrived in Paris?
Aarav: ....

5 **Pierre:** Are you going to be a pilot when you grow up?
Aarav: ....

A At 3 in the morning. I was sleeping when he left.

B I was eating breakfast. He arrived at 7 o'clock.

C He was at home.

(D) Of course he is!

E I don't know yet.

F He doesn't like to fly to Paris.

G He took the bus.

H To Paris. He usually flies to Paris on Mondays.

1 **Read the story. Was life easy eighty years ago?**

Grandma: Hi, Betty, what's that noise?

Betty: Oh, hi! It's Mom. She's vacuuming the living room.

Grandma: Lucky her! Our vacuum cleaner is broken. This morning I had to sweep the floor with a broom!

Betty: Well, with your new coffee maker, you could have a cup of coffee after that.

Grandma: Yes! And, because my washing machine was working, I didn't have to wash our clothes by hand, like my grandma had to do.

Betty: Was her life difficult?

Grandma: Yes, it was! Eighty years ago, there were electric vacuum cleaners and washing machines in some houses, but not in hers.

Betty: What about you? Could you call your friends when you were a child?

Grandma: Of course, Betty! But we couldn't take our phones to school like you do.

Betty: Did you have a TV?

Grandma: Yes, we did. But we couldn't change the channels from our couches. There were no remote controls!

2 **Read and circle T (*true*) or F (*false*).**

1	There were remote controls when Betty's grandma was young.	T / F
2	Betty's grandma used her washing machine this morning.	T / F
3	Betty's grandma could call her friends when she was young.	T / F
4	Betty's mom is doing the dishes.	T / F

3 **Read the text again. Underline sentences with *had to*, *didn't have to*, *could*, and *couldn't*. Then fill in the table.**

Grammar

Betty's grandmother	**had to** sweep the floor with a broom.
	.... wash her clothes by hand this morning.
	.... have a cup of coffee.
	couldn't take her phone to school when she was a child.

4 **Circle the correct answer.**

1 Fifty years ago, dishwashers weren't very common. People *had to / didn't have to* do the dishes after every meal.

2 After the electric vacuum cleaner became popular, people *didn't have to / had to* sweep floors. They *couldn't / could* clean a room in a few minutes.

3 The first microwave ovens were 1.5 meters tall and weighed 360 kilos. Families *could / couldn't* have one at home. Only some restaurants *could / couldn't* afford them.

5 **Read the sentences and decide which sentence talks about ability and which talks about obligation. Write A (ability) or O (obligation) next to the correct sentence.**

1 I could watch television, but I couldn't change the channels from the couch. ....

2 We had to help with the chores, so that our mom didn't have to work so hard. ....

6 **Complete the story with *had to, didn't have to, could,* or *couldn't*.**

When he was young, Elijah ____*couldn't*____ finish high school because he **(1)** _____ work to help his family. One of his teachers realized Elijah was very smart. She told him that she **(2)** _____ help him finish school, but Elijah **(3)** _____ come to her house every day after work and study. Elijah **(4)** _____ study a lot, but he managed to get high grades. Because of that, he **(5)** _____ get a scholarship and **(6)** _____ pay the tuition to go to college. He's a lawyer now!

7 **Imagine you are twenty years old. Tell a friend what you had to or didn't have to do and what you could or couldn't do when you were ten. Use the phrases in the box to help you.**

> clean my room   watch television   make the beds
> play at the park   do the laundry   take out the trash   do the dishes
> meet friends   use parents' computer   drive a car

When I was ten years old, I had to clean my room, but I didn't have to take out the trash.

I could meet my friends at the park, but I couldn't drive a car.

1 **Read Andrea's blog. What country is she visiting?**

Hi! Andrea here! My family and I finally landed after flying for over 20 hours from Rome, Italy. My parents wanted to sleep, but my brother and I wanted to see the city. The harbor is beautiful! We went on a boat tour and saw the Sydney Harbour Bridge, the Opera House, and the Royal Botanic Gardens.

♥   August 27   💬 →

Today we went on the Great Ocean Road. We drove 243 km from Torquay to Allansford. Now we're in the Blue Mountains National Park, 80 km west of Sydney. This is a photo of the Three Sisters. It's a rock formation above the Jamison Valley.

♥   August 29   💬 →

Yesterday we flew over the Great Barrier Reef. The reef is in the Coral Sea, and it consists of more than 2,900 coral reefs. Tomorrow we're visiting the Whitsunday Islands. They're 74 islands in the middle of the Great Barrier Reef.

♥   August 31   💬 →

2 **Read and complete with one word.**

Andrea and her family had to fly for over ...... *twenty* ...... *hours to get to Sydney.*

1 The Three Sisters is a rock formation above the Jamison ....

2 After the flight, Andrea's parents wanted to ....

3 Andrea .... over the Great Barrier Reef.

4 The family drove from Torquay to ....

3 **Read Andrea's blog again. Underline place names with the definite article (*the*) in red and place names with no article (*Ø*) in green.**

Grammar

Ø Oregon is in **the** USA. Ø Sydney is in Ø Australia.

The Three Sisters are three rocks in **the** Blue Mountains.

The Whitsunday Islands are in the middle of **the** Great Barrier Reef.

The Great Barrier Reef is in **the** Coral Sea.

The Sydney Opera House is next to **the** Royal Botanic Gardens.

An emu is taller than **a** kangaroo.

The kangaroo and **the** emu are typical Australian animals.

4 Circle the correct answer.

1 (The) / A Great Ocean Road is one of a / the most beautiful highways in Ø / the Australia.

2 A / The Great Barrier Reef covers an / a area of more than 2,900 coral reefs.

3 Andrea's family will take the / a Katoomba Scenic Railway to see a / the Jamison valley.

4 Not many people live in the / Ø Whitsunday Islands.

5 Ø / The Opera House isn't in a / Ø Allansford. It's in the / Ø Sydney.

5 Complete the rules below with Ø (no article) or the. Then write the correct letter in the box next to each rule.

A the Sydney Opera House, the Eiffel Tower, the Statue of Liberty

B Lima, Portugal, Vietnam, Cairo, France, New Zealand, Ottawa

C the Nile, the Blue Mountains, the Indian Ocean, the Easter Islands

D the Netherlands, the Philippines

1 ☐ With names of cities and most countries we use ....

2 ☐ With countries that have plural names we use ....

3 ☐ With geographical names (mountain ranges, groups of islands, seas, rivers, oceans) we use ....

4 ☐ With the names of landmarks we use ....

6 Complete the text with the/a/an or Ø.

Visit the amazing Southern Ocean coast!

The Twelve Apostles is (1) .... popular tourist attraction by (2) .... Great Ocean Road, in (3) .... Australia. It is (4) .... amazing group of rocks off the shore of (5) .... Port Campbell National Park.

This is a dangerous coast. Hundreds of ships sank near the coast of (6) .... Victoria. You can see their remains by following (7) .... Historic Shipwreck Trail. From the trail, you can follow the route to (8) .... Grampians, a mountain ridge in another national park.

7 Think of a well-known place in your country. Describe it to a friend. Your friend has to guess what place it is.

This place is in Egypt. It's by the Nile. It's near the Mediterranean Sea.

Is it a city?

Yes, it is.

Is it Cairo?

1 **Read the dialog. Why couldn't Sofia and her friends make a fire at the Boreang Campground?**

Lena: This is a great photo! Where did you take it?

Sofia: At the Blue Mountains National Park. I took it from the Katoomba Scenic Railway, the train which took us along the Jamison Valley. The views through its glass-roofed carriages are awesome!

Lena: And where's this?

Sofia: It's the Twelve Apostles by the Great Ocean Road. That's the highway that goes along the coast from Torquay to Allansford. This is the place where we started our journey to the Grampians.

Lena: Is that the park where you took the other pictures?

Sofia: Well, Jan is the person who took the pictures.

The Boreang Campground is the place where we wanted to spend the night in the Grampians National Park.

Lena: It looks great! What was it like?

Sofia: Well… we didn't stay long. There was a forest ranger that told us we couldn't light a fire to cook our meals.

Lena: That's weird! Why?

Sofia: Well, there is always a danger of starting a forest fire in Australia in the summer. The only food that we didn't have to cook were two sandwiches and an apple. We were very hungry, so we left early.

2 **Read and circle T (*true*) or F (*false*).**

1 Sofia and her friends were camping in the Grampians. T / F

2 You can see the Twelve Apostles from the Great Ocean Road. T / F

3 The Katoomba Scenic Railway has carriages which are glass-roofed. T / F

4 They could only eat food that they had cooked. T / F

5 Her friends told Sofia that she couldn't light a fire. T / F

Grammar

The Great Ocean Road is the highway **that** goes along the coast.

The train **which** took us along the Jamison Valley is the Katoomba Scenic Railway.

Jan is the person **who** took the pictures.

Boreang Campground was the place **where** they put up their tent.

3 Read the dialog again. Underline relative pronouns *that*, *which*, *who*, and *where*.

4 Circle the correct answer.

1 Karolina is the girl *who / which* went to Kenya.

2 Who's the person *which / that* is wearing binoculars?

3 This is the car *where / which* we rented in Berlin.

4 Is that the hotel *which / where* you stayed in Lisbon?

5 I don't think the man *who / where* is behind you in this photo is a forest ranger.

6 Let's look for a place *where / that* we can eat dinner.

5 Can you use both relative pronouns in the sentences? Write *Yes* or *No*.

1 This is the forest ranger *who/that* told us we couldn't light a fire. ....

2 The strange building *that/which* looks like a ship is the Sydney Opera House. ....

3 The Whitsunday Islands is the place *where/that* we went snorkeling. ....

6 Complete the sentences.

This is a photo of the friends ___that/who___ went to Madagascar last January.

1 The campsite _____ is in the Grampians National Park is amazing.

2 Emilia is the red-haired girl _____ is standing in front of Antoni.

3 The Great Barrier Reef is a place _____ you can see a lot of tropical fish.

4 The tall woman _____ is next to Marta is one of the park guides.

5 Whitehaven Beach is the beach _____ the sand is white.

7 Describe some of the nouns from the box using *who*, *which*, *that*, or *where*.

calculator science ~~my dad~~
ice cream parlor my grandma
beach laptop library pizza
firefighter pencil park

My dad's the person who drives me to school every day.

1 ....

....

2 ....

....

3 ....

....

8 **Look at the pictures and find six differences. Tell a friend what differences you found in Picture B.**

A

B

In Picture A there's a fox behind a tree.

There isn't a fox in Picture B.

He taught himself to use a compass

1 **Read the dialog. What did Fredo do on Sunday?**

Ines: Hi, Fredo! I didn't see you on Sunday. Where were you?

Fredo: Hi, Ines! I was orienteering.

Ines: Orienteering? What's that?

Fredo: Well, it's a kind of race. You have to go from one site to the next one using a compass and a map. How you reach the control sites is up to you. The first person to finish is the winner.

Ines: It sounds easy.

Fredo: Well, it isn't! I had to teach myself to use a compass and to read a map before I could participate. I also trained myself to walk five kilometers in an hour. A race for beginners takes about two hours.

Ines: Do you need any special equipment?

Fredo: You basically need walking shoes, a hat, and a bottle of water. The only special equipment is a compass and a whistle.

Ines: What's the whistle for?

Fredo: You need a whistle in case you get lost or hurt yourself. My brother, Santi, hurt himself at a race last month. Luckily, he had his whistle and could call for help.

2 **Read and write *Yes* or *No*.**

1 The control sites are between the beginning and the end of the race. ....

2 People can use the whistle to call for help when they get lost. ....

3 Fredo taught himself how to use a compass after he did the race. ....

4 Fredo trained himself to walk a kilometer in an hour. ....

5 In orienteering, participants go from one point to another using a map and a compass. ....

Grammar

I hurt **myself** when I was playing soccer.

Did **you** train **yourself** to run five kilometers in 30 minutes?

He taught **himself** to use a compass.

She hurt **herself** and had to use the whistle to call for help.

My dog can't run. **It** hurt **itself** when it stepped on broken glass.

We trained **ourselves** to walk five kilometers in an hour.

You enjoyed **yourselves** a lot at the end-of-race party.

They taught **themselves** to use a compass.

3 Read the dialog again and underline sentences with reflexive pronouns (*myself*, *yourself*, etc.).

4 Circle the correct answer.

1 Fredo taught *himself / him* to use a compass. No one helped him.

2 Alice woke up and dressed *myself / herself*.

3 Did you enjoy *yourself / you* at the party?

4 I cut *me / myself* when I was making a sandwich.

5 We had to dry *yourself / ourselves* after swimming in the pool.

6 They should train *themself / themselves* to run ten kilometers in under an hour.

7 My cat taught *itself / myself* to open the door.

8 Are you hungry? You can help *herself / yourself* to some pizza.

5 Read the sentences and answer the questions.

1 After washing himself, Pablo dressed himself.

2 After washing him, Pablo dressed him.

A Did Pablo wash and dress another person in sentence one?

B Did Pablo wash and dress another person in sentence two?

6 Complete the sentences with the correct reflexive pronoun.

1 I never cook .... breakfast in the mornings.

2 Stefan always enjoys .... at parties.

3 David, be careful! You'll cut .... !

4 My brother and I have to teach .... to play the piano. Dad won't do it.

5 Hank, tell your sister to get out of the cold water and dry .... She'll catch a cold!

6 You and Natalia are old enough to make sandwiches ....

7 Think about what you and your family did last week and write sentences. Use the phrases in the box or your own ideas.

cut   cook/dinner   dress
enjoy/at the movies   hurt
teach/to draw
train/to use left hand   shave

I cooked myself dinner on Wednesday.

1 My dad ....

....

2 ....

....

3 ....

....

4 ....

....

5 ....

....

She's been a doctor for five years

1 Read the dialog. Does Elif want to be a scientist?

Elif: Hi, Auntie! Can I ask you some questions? It's for a school project.

Aunt Fatma: Of course! What do you want to know?

Elif: What's your job?

Aunt Fatma: I'm a scientist. I work at the laboratory at Green Cedar Hospital.

Elif: How long have you worked there?

Aunt Fatma: Since I graduated from college. That was three years ago.

Elif: Where do you live?

Aunt Fatma: I have lived in an apartment near the hospital for the last two years.

Elif: Did you live in a house before that?

Aunt Fatma: No, I haven't lived in a house since I started college.

Elif: Do you have many friends at work?

Aunt Fatma: Of course!

Elif: Who's your best friend?

Aunt Fatma: Asya. She's also a scientist. We've been friends since we were students at college. She's been my friend for seven years.

Elif: I want to work in a hospital one day, too. But I want to be a doctor.

Aunt Fatma: My friend Miray is a doctor. She's been a doctor for five years. You should talk to her.

2 Read and complete with one or two words.

1 Fatma's apartment is .... the hospital.

2 Fatma's been friends with Asya for ....

3 Elif's aunt is a ....

4 Fatma has worked at the hospital since she ....

3 Read the dialog again. Underline sentences in Present Perfect (_have_/_has_ + past participle). Then fill in the table.

Grammar

I/You/We/They **have** .... in this apartment **for** two years.	I/You/We/They **haven't** .... in an apartment **since** 2015.
He/She/It **has** .... at the hospital **since** 2005.	He/She/It .... **lived** in a house **since** he/she/it started college.
.... you **met** my friend Theresa?	Yes, I .... / No, I ....

19

4 Circle the correct answer.

1 Carlos and I *been / have been* friends since we were children.

2 How long *you have worked / have you worked* at the bank?

3 We have lived in this house *since / for* twelve years.

4 My parents have *knew / known* each other for sixteen years.

5 Mrs. Beck has taught at our school *for / since* 2012.

6 I'm hungry! I *haven't ate / haven't eaten* for three hours!

7 Agatha has worked in the bakery *for / since* she finished high school.

8 I haven't seen my cousins *for / since* six months. I miss them!

5 Read and complete the sentences. Then answer the questions.

1 I have known Anna .... we started school.

2 She has been my friend .... seven years.

A Are the actions still taking place?

B When do we use *since*?

C When do we use *for*?

6 Complete the text with the correct form of the verbs.

Hi! My name's Theo. I was tagged by my friends to write six random facts about myself. So here they are:

I *have lived* (live) in Chicago since I was born. I **(1)** .... (know) my best friend for seven years. I **(2)** .... (not/eat) chocolate since last week. I love movies, but I **(3)** .... (not/be) to the movie theater this year. My parents **(4)** .... (be) married for fifteen years. A squirrel **(5)** .... (live) in our attic for five years now.

7 Now write some facts about yourself. Use the phrases in the box to help you.

> live in   know my best friend
> have a pet   study English
> learn a poem by heart
> run in the park   travel by bus

1 .... since
   ....

2 .... for
   ....

3 ....
   ....

4 ....
   ....

We've already seen the Kechak fire dance

1 Read Vedran's blog posts. Where have the boys traveled to?

My friend Diego and I are going to travel for a year before starting college. We're leaving in a week, but we've already decided which countries to visit. Follow us around the world!

March 21
We're in Bali! We've already seen the Kechak fire dance at Uluwatu Temple.

It was awesome! The Balinese have performed the dance for over 80 years.

March 10
We've been in Istanbul since Monday. We have already seen so many things! This is a view of the Blue Mosque. We haven't been to the Topkapi Palace Museum yet. We're going tomorrow. We want to see its fabulous jewel collection.

April 3
Is this China? No! This is San Francisco. We arrived in the United States

two hours ago. This is the view from our hotel window. We haven't had time to walk around the city yet.

2 Read and answer the questions.

1 Have they visited the Topkapi Palace Museum yet? ....

2 Who is Vedran traveling with?
....

3 What city haven't the boys walked around yet? ....

4 Where did the boys see the Kechak fire dance? ....

3 Read Vedran's blog again. Underline sentences in Present Perfect with _already_ and _yet_.

Grammar

The boys have **already** seen many things in Istanbul.

Have they visited the Topkapi Palace **yet**?

No, they haven't visited it **yet**.

4 Circle the correct answer.

1 I have _already_ / _yet_ decided what countries to visit.

2 Have you seen the Chinese fishing nets in Cochin _yet_ / _already_?

3 The boys have _yet_ / _already_ visited the Uluwatu Temple.

4 We haven't visited San Francisco _already_ / _yet_.

5 — Read the sentences and complete the rules with *yet* or *already*.

1 They have already finished their homework.

2 They haven't finished their homework yet.

3 Have they finished their homework yet?

We use .... when something has happened.

We use .... when something hasn't happened and in questions.

We use .... at the end of a sentence.

We use .... in the middle of a sentence.

6 Read Vedran's blog post about his visit to San Francisco. Complete with the correct form of the verbs and *already* or *yet* when necessary.

I ...*haven't posted*... (not/post) anything since last week, but I **(1)** .... (not/forget) about you. San Francisco is fantastic! There are so many things to see!

This morning Diego and I are making a list of the places we **(2)** .... (visit/already) and those we **(3)** .... (not/visit/yet). We **(4)** .... (be/already) to so many places that it is difficult to remember where we were. Luckily, we **(5)** .... (take) a lot of pictures since we arrived.

We **(6)** .... (be/already) to the Golden Gate Bridge. It's an awesome view!

We **(7)** .... (become/already) experts in traveling by cable car. This morning we are going to take one from Chinatown to Pier 39 to see the sea lions sunbathing. To our surprise, we **(8)** .... (get lost/yet)!

7 — Tell your friend three things you have already done and three things you haven't done yet.

I have already been to Peru and India.

I haven't won the school basketball championship yet.

8 Complete the email. Write one word for each space.

Dear Hiro,

I'm sorry I haven't written ___for___ so long. Guess what! We've moved to a new house! I live **(1)** _____ San Diego now. Things **(2)** _____ been a bit crazy lately. My mom has **(3)** _____ redecorated the kitchen three times! And you know how **(4)** _____ my dad loves his car. He hasn't washed it **(5)** _____ we moved in. He's too busy helping Mom! Annika and Jack **(6)** _____ already unpacked all their things. They have so **(7)** _____ toys! They're only seven so they **(8)** _____ do it by themselves. I **(9)** _____ to help them, so I haven't finished cleaning my room **(10)** _____ .

Love,

Ethan

9 Look at the pictures. Write about this story. Write 20 or more words.

....

....

....

....

....

....

1 **Read this article in a blog post. Then do the quiz.**

● ● ●

Things children do before they're 12
We asked some boys and girls these questions.

Have you ever...	Yes	No
1) climbed a tree?		
2) camped out in the wild?		
3) flown a kite?		
4) run around in the rain?		
5) caught a fish with a net?		
6) looked for shells at the beach?		
7) visited an island?		
8) watched the sun come up?		
9) fed a bird from your hand?		

Here are some of the answers.

Piotr, 11 ½: No, I have never climbed a tree and I have never camped out in the wild. But I have visited an island and I have fed a bird from my hand.

Alicia, 11: My parents love camping, so I have camped out in the wild many times. Of course, I have looked for shells at the beach and I have caught fish with a net. It was the most fun I have ever had!

What about you? Have you ever done any of these things?

2 **Read and complete with one word.**

1 Alicia has caught _____ with a net.

2 Piotr has never climbed a _____ .

3 Alicia's parents like _____ .

4 Piotr has visited an _____ .

Grammar

I have **never** flown a kite.

This is the most fun I have **ever** had!

Have you _____ flown a kite?

Yes, I have.   No, I haven't.

3 **Read the article again. Underline one sentence with _ever_ and one sentence with _never_. Then fill in the table.**

4 **Circle the correct answer.**

1   A: Have you _ever / never_ sailed on a boat?

   B: Yes, I have. But I have _never / ever_ sailed on a boat in a storm.

2   A: So, your dad's a pilot! Have you _never / ever_ been on a plane?

   B: Of course! Many times! But I have _ever / never_ flown a plane.

5 Read the examples and discuss the questions with a friend.

1 Have you ever been to Thailand?

2 She has never eaten baklava.

3 It's the first time I have ever tried pizza.

4 Hawaii is the most beautiful place I have ever visited.

A When do we use *ever*?

B When do we use *never*?

6 Read the interview. Complete with the correct form of the verbs and *ever* or *never* when necessary.

Journalist: **(1)** _____ you _____ (want/ever) to do an activity with your whole family? That's what Miguel's family does every weekend. How did you get the idea of going mountain biking with the whole family?

Miguel: I **(2)** _____ (enjoy) doing physical activities since I was a child. But I also wanted to spend time with my family. Since we live in a small town up in the mountains, we used to go hiking every Saturday morning. But… I **(3)** _____ (enjoy/never) walking.

Journalist: I can see how that could be a problem.

Miguel: And then my wife reminded me that I had a good mountain bike in the shed. I **(4)** _____ (ride) a bike since I was six, and so have my children. So, here we are!

Journalist: **(5)** _____ you _____ (feel/ever) too tired to bike?

Miguel: Well, yes. **(6)** I _____ (feel) like staying in bed many times! But my children **(7)** _____ (let/never) me do that! And it's good to have an activity we can all do together.

7 Has your friend ever done any of these activities? Ask and answer.

climb the Eiffel Tower	play a dangerous sport	make a sandcastle
swim with sharks	ride a horse	play baseball

Have you ever ridden a horse?

No, I haven't. Have you ever climbed the Eiffel Tower?

8 📝 **Read the sentences about a family that goes hiking together. Choose the best word (A, B, or C) for each space.**

Our family has   B   hiking for the last three years.

A   going   (B) gone   C   went

1   Mom and Dad .... played lots of sports together since they got married.

  A has   **B** had   **C** have

2   They only .... to find one activity which my sister and I enjoyed.

  A had   **B** has   **C** have

3   And they have .... it. We all like hiking.

  A find   **B** found   **C** founded

4   We have been hiking every weekend .... the last three months.

  A for   **B** since   **C** already

5   We have .... had more fun in our lives!

  A ever   **B** yet   **C** never

1 **Read Ahmad's email. There is a place in New York where he hasn't been yet. What is it?**

Hi Grandpa!

We started our trip a month ago in Alaska, where we took a photo of a momma bear and her cubs. That was very exciting! Then we flew to California and started our road trip. We've already visited the Rocky Mountains National Park in Colorado. It's one of the most beautiful places I have ever seen! A backpacker told us to take the Waterfalls Hike. We've already been to Adams Falls, too.

We've also visited Mount Rushmore in South Dakota. We saw the heads of George Washington, Thomas Jefferson, Theodore Roosevelt, and Abraham Lincoln there. Gutzon Borglum and 400 men worked from 1927 to 1941 to make this monument. Millions of people have visited it since then.

We arrived in New York on Friday morning and we have already taken so many photos! We haven't been to the Statue of Liberty yet. But we have already been to the Metropolitan Museum and to Central Park. We were there on Saturday.

Love,

Ahmad

2 **Read and circle T (*true*) or F (*false*).**

1   Ahmad saw the heads of four American presidents at Mount Rushmore.   T / F

2   Not many people have visited Mount Rushmore.   T / F

3   They took a photo of the bears in California.   T / F

4   A backpacker told them to go to Adams Falls.   T / F

Grammar

Past Simple		Present Perfect	
They **were** in California a month ago.		They **have been** to Alaska.	
Harry **didn't visit** Florida.		She **hasn't visited** Mount Rushmore yet.	
Did you **arrive** in New York on Friday?		**Have** you already **been** to Central Park?	
Yes, we **did**.	No, we **didn't**.	Yes, we **have**.	No, we **haven't**.

3 **Read Ahmad's email again. Underline verbs in Past Simple in yellow and verbs in Present Perfect in green.**

4 Circle the correct answer.

1   They *have seen / saw* a bear family when they were in Alaska.

2   Millions of people *visited / have visited* Mount Rushmore over the last 70 years.

3   I *have bought / bought* new hiking boots last year.

4   They *arrived / have arrived* in Madrid last Monday morning.

5 Color time expressions used in Past Simple yellow. Color time expressions used in Present Perfect green. Then answer the questions.

never	two weeks ago	ever	since	for	last week

in 2010	yet	yesterday	already

A   When do we use Past Simple?

B   When do we use Present Perfect?

6 Complete the sentences with the correct form of the verbs.

We _____*left*_____ (leave) Turkey six weeks ago. We talk to our families over the internet every day, so we **(1)** _____ (not start) missing home yet.

Yesterday, we **(2)** _____ (visit) the Statue of Liberty. In the afternoon, we **(3)** _____ (go) to Yankee Stadium. No, we aren't baseball fans. But we **(4)** _____ (want) to see New York City FC play the New York Red Bulls. The NYCFC **(5)** _____ (adapt) Yankee Stadium and they **(6)** _____ (play) soccer there since 2015.

7 Ask a friend whether he/she has done these activities. If yes, find out when this happened.

win a prize

meet someone famous

cook breakfast for your mom

sleep in a tent   make a cake

Have you ever won a prize?

Yes, I have.

When did you win it?

1 Read the article. What can people do to order food?

Click a meal!

How many times have you felt like eating, but you didn't want to cook?

Nowadays, you don't have to leave home to have your favorite meal. You can order it from a restaurant and ask them to deliver it. But this hasn't always been so.

The first food delivery service was the Women's Volunteer Service in the United Kingdom. During the Second World War, these women delivered food to bombed homes.

The first city in the United States that set up a food delivery service was Philadelphia. Thanks to this service, people who were old or ill could receive their food at home. Some restaurant owners realized that they could make money delivering food. Chicago was the first city which had a pizza delivery service. Quickly, this service spread to the whole of the United States.

These days, you don't have to call a restaurant to order your favorite dish. You can order it online. You only have to click on a restaurant, see the menu, and order. Within minutes, your favorite food will be at your table. You'll still have to do the dishes, though!

2 Read and answer the questions. Use no more than four words.

1 What was the first food delivery service? ....

2 Which city had the first food delivery service in the United States? ....

3 Which city first started delivering pizza in the United States?

....

4 What's the newest way of ordering food? ....

5 What chore do you still have to do? ....

3 Read the article again and underline sentences with relative pronouns.

4 Circle the correct answer.

My mom usually cooks breakfast, lunch, and dinner by **(1)** *ourselves / herself* on weekdays. But on Saturdays and Sundays, my brother and I cook some meals **(2)** *himself / ourselves*. "Be careful with the knives! Don't cut **(3)** *yourself / yourselves*," Mom always tells us. But we are good cooks. My brother taught **(4)** *himself / herself* to make pizza, and I taught **(5)** *myself / ourselves* to make scrambled eggs. My dad doesn't cook, but he usually helps **(6)** *herself / himself* to the food first!

5 Complete the diary entry with *had to, didn't have to, could,* or *couldn't.*

February 15, 1954

Mom's at the hospital because Jimmy, my little brother, was born on Friday. She left Helen and me a list of the chores we ___*had to*___ do.

On Saturday, I **(1)** _____ do the laundry. Helen didn't have to do any chores, so she **(2)** _____ play outside.

Unfortunately, Helen broke her arm, so she **(3)** _____ help me iron Dad's shirts on Sunday.

Helen **(4)** _____ make the beds today, but her arm hurt, so Aunt Sylvia came and helped us. Aunt Sylvia did the dishes today, so I **(5)** _____ do them.

6 Add the definite pronoun *the* when necessary.

1 We didn't visit _____ Houses of Parliament when we were in _____ London.

2 _____ Alps are the longest mountain range in _____ Europe.

3 Alice lives in _____ England, which is part of _____ United Kingdom.

4 This summer we went to _____ Easter Island, in the middle of _____ Pacific Ocean.

5 Which is _____ longest river on _____ Earth: _____ Nile or _____ Amazon?

7 Connect the two parts of the sentences using *who, which, that,* or *where.*

A
~~A forest ranger is a person~~
The Topkapı Palace is the museum
A bicycle is the means of transport
A scientist is a person
Orienteering is an activity

B
I use every day to go to school
you can see a fabulous jewel collection
~~protects trees and animals from damage~~
doesn't require much special equipment
works in a hospital or a laboratory

A forest ranger is a person who protects trees and animals from damage.

1 The Topkapı Palace is the museum _____ .

2 _____ .

3 _____ .

4 _____ .

8 Read the story. Choose a word from the box. Write the correct word next to numbers 1–5.

~~ranger~~ has earlier later themselves
himself hospital late have the

Sally and her family live in a small town next to a large river. Sally's dad is a forest _ranger_ at the national park. Her mom is a nurse at **(1)** _____ town hospital.

In the mornings, Sally has to help her mom cook breakfast for the family. She doesn't have to dress her two younger brothers or comb their hair. They can do that **(2)** _____ , but she has to walk to school with them. She always complains because she is usually **(3)** _____ .

"They are too slow, Mom!" she says.

"You need to leave **(4)** _____ , Sally," her mom always answers.

One morning, Sally's dad said "OK! Get in my truck! Today, I'll drive you all to school."

"Are you sure, Bert? The children **(5)** _____ to do some exercise every day. Walking to school is good for them!" said Mom.

"Well, as of tomorrow I'm leaving for the park at five in the morning. I don't think they'll want to ride with me then."

(6) Now, choose the best name for the story. Check one box.

Getting up at 5 is good for you. ☐

Exercise is important. ☐

One happy morning ☐

1 Read the quiz. Circle the correct answers.

What are the objects that we use every day made of?

The objects we use in our everyday life are made of different materials.
Do you know their names?

1 This box is made of _____ .

  A glass   Ⓒ wood

  B plastic   D metal

2 What material is this castle made of?
It's made of _____ .

  A stone   C metal

  B glass   D rubber

3 This can is made of _____ .
It isn't made of rubber.

  A metal   C glass

  B wood   D plastic

4 Is this wall very strong?
Yes, it is. It's made of _____ .

  A wood   C plastic

  B metal   D bricks

5 You can walk in the rain in these boots.
They're made of _____ .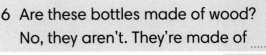

  A stone   C rubber

  B metal   D wool

6 Are these bottles made of wood?
No, they aren't. They're made of _____ .

  A glass   C plastic

  B rubber   D metal

7 This teacup is made of _____ .

  A wood   C metal

  B plastic   D glass

8 I wear these socks in winter.
They are made of _____ .

  A rubber   C plastic

  B wool   D glass

2 Read and answer the questions.

1 What's made of metal?

2 Is there any coffee in the cup?

3 What color are the bottles made of plastic?

4 Do people wear rubber boots when it's sunny?

3 Read the quiz again. Underline questions with _made of_. Then fill in the table.

Grammar

The teacup **is made of** glass.
It _____ **made of** wood.

The socks _____ **made of** wool.
They **aren't made of** plastic.

What **are** the boots **made of**?
They _____ **made of** rubber.

_____ the wall **made of** bricks?

Yes, it **is**.   No, it **isn't**.

4 Circle the correct answer.

1 A: What a nice vase! Who (made) / make it?

B: I'm glad you like it! My mom **(1)** *makes / made* it.

A: What is it made **(2)** *of / with*?

B: It's made **(3)** *in / of* clay.

2 C: What an interesting object! Where was it **(4)** *making / made*?

D: It was **(5)** *made / make* in China.

C: What **(6)** *is / was* it made of?

D: It's made **(7)** *of / in* copper.

5 Read the sentences. Is their meaning similar or different? Does it say who made the objects? Is it important?

1 Aki makes leather boots. He's very good at it.

2 These boots are made of leather. They're very expensive.

3 Francis makes glass jewelry. He's very talented.

4 This jewelry is made of glass. It's so pretty.

6 Look at the pictures and complete the sentences.

1 This bucket is .... plastic.

2 But the gloves .... of rubber.

3 The Eiffel Tower .... of iron.

4 What are those T-shirts made of?

They .... made .... cotton.

7 Look around the classroom and find things made of different materials. Ask your friend to guess what the things are made of.

What is your T-shirt made of?

It's made of cotton. My turn. What's this pencil made of?

1 **Read the dialog. Why has Mrs. Carter changed the class schedule?**

Tommy:	Come on, Lizzy! We'll be late again! Class starts in five minutes!
Lizzy:	I'm sorry! I can't walk any faster.

Mrs. Carter:	Good morning, Tommy! Class starts at 8:15 every morning!
Tommy:	Sorry, Mrs. Carter. My little sister walks too slowly.
Mrs. Carter:	You should leave home earlier, then. Class, please remember that Ms. Perez, your Spanish teacher, is sick. So we have changed our schedule for this week.
Jorje:	When do we have music, Mrs. Carter?
Mrs. Carter:	Tomorrow, from 9:55, instead of Spanish.
Tommy:	And when do we have science?
Mrs. Carter:	On Wednesday. Miss Young can't come earlier, so science starts at 10:55.
Mei:	When do we have P.E.?
Mrs. Carter:	On Thursday, as usual. P.E. doesn't change.
Peter:	What about our school trip to the Science Museum on Friday?
Mrs. Carter:	Our school trip doesn't change. The school bus leaves at 7:30. Please make sure you're here on time because we cannot wait. Remember that the museum opens on Friday only for us.

2 **Read and complete the sentences.**

1 The P.E. class is on
.... , as usual.

2 The Spanish teacher is called
....

3 Class starts at ....
every morning.

4 The bus can't wait for the students
who are ....

3 **Read the dialog again. Underline sentences in Present Simple which talk about future events.**

Grammar

The music class **starts** at 9:55.

They **go** to the museum on Friday.

When **do** you **have** music this week?

4 **Circle the correct answer.**

1 A: What time does the school bus
leave *next Friday / last Friday*?

B: It *leaves / leave* at 7:30 and it
arrives / arriving at the museum
at 8:30.

2 The theater *open / opens* at
6 o'clock and the play *begins /
beginning* at 7:30.

5 Read the sentences and circle to make the rule.

1 Hurry up! The movie starts in five minutes!

2 The mall opens at 7 o'clock.

We use Present Simple to talk about *past / future* events which *are / aren't* scheduled.

6 Complete the text with the correct form of the verbs.

New classes at Maple Road Sports Center!

Maple Road Sports Center is pleased to announce that starting next Monday we're offering a soccer academy and new dance classes.

Do you want your child to learn to play soccer? Would you like to play indoor soccer?

Classes at the Soccer Academy for 6 to15 year olds **(1)** .... (start) on Monday evening. Classes **(2)** .... (last) from 5 p.m. to 7 p.m.

Players aged 16 and over can play in the indoor soccer league, which **(3)** .... (begin) next Friday evening at 8:15. Practice **(4)** .... (end) at 9:45.

Are you interested in our dance classes?

The Dance Academy **(5)** .... (start) on Saturday morning for children aged 3–12. Classes **(6)** .... (begin) at 9.

7 Look at Santiago's calendar. Write sentences about his week in your notebook.

Monday	Tuesday	Wednesday	Thursday	Friday	Saturday
science test!	no English today, music instead	5 p.m. school tennis tournament	3 p.m. audition for the school play starts	bike trip with class; we leave at 10 a.m.	10 a.m. first swimming lesson (catch bus at 9:30)

Santiago has a science test on Monday.

8 Carlos is talking to his friend, Julio, about the weekend. What does Carlos say to Julio?

Read the dialog and choose the best answer. Write a letter (A–H) for each answer. You do not need to use all the letters.

Julio: *Hi, Carlos. It's Julio.*
Carlos: *G*

1 **Julio:** Yes, that's why I'm calling. I was at soccer practice.
Carlos: ....

2 **Julio:** Every Saturday morning from 8:30 to 12:45.
Carlos: ....

3 **Julio:** I don't mind, I love soccer. Why did you call me?
Carlos: ....

4 **Julio:** Are you going to be in it?
Carlos: ....

5 **Julio:** Sure! Where should we meet?
Carlos: ....

A I don't think I would like to get up so early on the weekend.

B Well, I wanted to talk about our school's climbing competition next Friday.

C It's too late for me!

D Oh! I forgot you were on the school soccer team. How often do you practice?

E Yes, I am. It takes place at Climbat. Do you want to come, too?

F Come to my house at 11 a.m. My dad will drive us.

G Hi. I called you several times! Did you get my text?

H At 11 o'clock.

14 Robots may change people's lives

1 Read the dialog. Will people work in the future?

Mrs. Jones: To sum up, I'm an engineer and I make robots which may change people's lives.

Teacher: Thanks, Mrs. Jones. That was a very interesting talk. Students, do you have any questions?

Bella: I do! Will we work in the future, or might robots do all jobs?

Mrs. Jones: Robots may do some of the simple jobs people do. But there will always be jobs that only people can do, like being a teacher, or a doctor, or even making robots. So, some jobs might go to robots only, others may change, but people will always have to work.

Saleh: Will we come to school on a driverless bus next year?

Mrs. Jones: Well, in the future, students may come to school on a driverless bus. But I don't think this will happen next year.

Ralph: Might engineers make a robot that is more intelligent than people?

Mrs. Jones: Not right now. We may make robots that travel to the stars, in fact we already can, but there will always have to be engineers like me... or you in a few years... to tell them what to do.

2 Read and circle T (*true*) or F (*false*).

1	Engineers may make robots that are more intelligent than people.	T / F
2	In the future, robots may do all the jobs that people do.	T / F
3	Buses will still need a driver in the near future.	T / F
4	Robots can make new robots.	T / F

3 Read the dialog again. Underline sentences with <u>may</u> and <u>might</u>. Then fill in the table.

Grammar

Robots **may** change people's lives.

Robots _____ do simple jobs.

Might robots travel to the stars? Yes, they _____ . In fact, some already do.

Might engineers make a robot that is more intelligent than people?

Well, perhaps they _____ , but not for many years.

4 Circle the correct answer.

Our future! (By Tim)

I think in 200 years we *may* / *might* have colonies on Mars and the Moon. Conditions there are very hard, so the colonies **(1)** *may* / *might* be very small. Because there once was water on Mars, the Martian colony **(2)** *may* / *might* be more successful. Traveling to Mars **(3)** *may* / *might* still be very expensive. People **(4)** *may* / *might* fly to very distant stars, like Alpha Centauri, but I don't think this will be possible for many years.

5 Read the sentences and answer the questions.

1 People may travel in driverless cars in the near future.

2 People might find life on another planet one day.

A Which sentence is about something that is possible? ....

B Which one is about something that has little possibility of happening? ....

6 Complete the text with *may* or *might*.

Which of these things do you think will be more or less possible in 2120?

1 NASA is planning to land people on Mars in 2030. So, there .... be a colony on Mars after that.

2 People already interconnect via the internet, so students .... not have to go to school at all in the future. They will all learn from home.

3 After traveling to Mars or the Moon, people .... travel to the nearest star at the speed of light. But scientists think this won't be possible before 2200.

7 When do you think this will happen? Discuss with a friend.

travel to Mars   use a robot to wash windows   find life on other planets

travel in a driverless bus   have a robot as a teacher   clone a person

I think people might travel to Mars in 2100.

Well, there's already a rover on Mars, so I think this may happen in the next 20 years.

You don't serve pizza, do you?

1 **Read the dialog. What did the boys order for lunch?**

Emil: I'm hungry. It's almost noon. Let's get something to eat.

Akoni: Good idea! There's a good fast food restaurant at the mall, isn't there?

Waitress: Hi! What can I get for you?

Akoni: You don't serve pizza, do you?

Waitress: No, we only serve burgers and hot dogs.

Emil: I'd like a cheeseburger with a fried egg. It comes with fries, doesn't it?

Waitress: You can choose fries or a salad.

Akoni: A salad is healthier than fries, isn't it?

Emil: Yes, but I don't want to go hungry, do I? I'll have the fries, please.

Waitress: Would you like a soda or a milkshake with your burger?

Emil: Soda, with ice and a slice of lemon, please.

Waitress: What about you?

Akoni: A deluxe hot dog for me. You have special toppings, don't you?

Waitress: You can have a topping of cream cheese, pineapple, and green onions, or one of mustard, onions, cucumbers, and tomatoes. Deluxe hot dogs come with a salad and fries. You can also have a milkshake or a soda.

Akoni: I'll have cream cheese, pineapple, and green onions with my hot dog, and a milkshake, please. This place is very nice, isn't it?

Emil: And it isn't expensive, is it?

2 **Read and write *Yes* or *No*.**

1 It's almost 12 o'clock. ....

2 Emil will drink lemon juice with ice. ....

3 The restaurant is cheap. ....

4 The restaurant serves pizza. ....

5 Emil can have fries or a salad with his cheeseburger. ....

3 **Read the dialog again. Underline sentences with question tags. Then fill in the table.**

Grammar

I don't want to go hungry, **do I?**

You serve fast food, **don't you?**

He/She wants a pizza, **doesn't he/she?**

This restaurant isn't expensive, ... **it?**

We like burgers, **don't** .... ?

You don't serve pizza, **do you?**

Hamburgers come with fries, **don't they?**

4 Circle the correct answer.

1 **A:** Making a strawberry milkshake isn't very difficult, *is she / is it?*

B: You have all the ingredients, **(1)** *don't they / don't you?*

A: I think so. I need vanilla ice cream, milk, and some strawberries, **(2)** *do I / don't I?*

B: That's right! And you also need a blender!

2 **C:** Hi Mom! I'm really hungry! There's some pizza in the fridge **(3)** *isn't it / isn't there?*

D: There's only jalapeño pizza left. You don't like spicy food, **(4)** *do you / don't you?*

C: No, I don't. There aren't any muffins from breakfast, **(5)** *are there / aren't there?*

D: Sorry, your brother ate all the muffins. But you like pancakes, **(6)** *do you / don't you?* I can make you some.

5 Read and complete the sentences. Then answer the questions.

1 You're hungry, aren't you?
She isn't very tired, ... she?

2 They like hot dogs, ... they?
He doesn't want to go hungry, does he?

3 There are some cupcakes, aren't there? There isn't a cake in the fridge, ... there?

A When is the question tag negative?

B When is it affirmative?

6 Complete the sentences with the correct question tags.

Emilio likes cheeseburgers,
*   doesn't he?*
....

1 Your mom doesn't want you to eat junk food, ... ?

2 I don't have to redo my homework, ... ?

3 They only serve fish at this restaurant, ... ?

4 You aren't very good at math, ... ?

5 Aunt Dot's good at cooking, ... ?

6 Your dog is named Spot, ... ?

7 How well do you know your friend? Make sentences with question tags to check the following.

his/her age   play an instrument

like milkshakes   like red

know how to make an omelette

like pineapple on pizza

own a hamster   dance well

have a sister/brother

You play the trumpet, don't you?

Yes, I do. My turn. You don't like red, do you?

8 These pictures tell a story. It's called "Why don't we have pizza tonight?" Look at the pictures first. Dad has called the pizzeria. A man is taking his order. Dad's asking for four pizzas. Work with a friend and continue the story.

They're such a bargain!

1 Read the dialog. What are the boys looking for?

Mom: This shopping mall is such a busy place! Make sure you don't get lost.

Adam: Oh, Mom! Marcel and I are 15! We can go to the men's section while you go shopping with the girls. We can meet here at 12 o'clock.

Mom: That's such a good idea! Make sure you're here on time, boys. Do you know where you want to go, Laura?

Laura: I'd like to look for a new dress.

Mom: Great! Marta and I need some jeans, don't we?

Marta: Yes, Mom. Laura, look at those dresses! They're such lovely shades of blue!

Laura: Oh, they're so pretty!

Mom: They are, but look at the prices! This is such an expensive store.

....

Adam: What are we looking for?

Marcel: I need new sneakers.

Adam: There are plenty of shoe stores on this level. Look! That store has a sale! What about those sneakers?

Marcel: Awesome! Let's go in! Hi! I'd like to try on the green sneakers, please.

Assistant: What size are you?

Marcel: I wear size 9.

Assistant: Here you are.

Adam: They're such a great color!

Assistant: And they're half price.

Marcel: They're such a bargain! I'll take them.

2 Read and answer the questions.

1 What are the girls looking at?

....

2 Are the dresses the girls like cheap? ....

3 What time do the boys have to be back? ....

4 What size does Marcel wear?

....

5 Why are the sneakers such a bargain? ....

Grammar

The shopping mall is **such a** busy place.

This is **such an** amazing store.

Those are **such** pretty dresses.

3 Read the dialog again. Underline sentences with _such_ and _such a/an_.

4 Circle the correct answer.

1 I saw a documentary about penguins. It's *such a / such* great movie!

2 My dad doesn't want to lend his new car to my older sister. She's *such a / such* bad driver!

3 I like going to Phil's for dinner. His parents are *such a / such* nice people.

4 I don't think coming to this restaurant was *such / such a* great idea. The food is horrible!

5 Anita is so elegant. She always wears *such a / such* nice clothes.

6 It's *such an / such a* interesting book.

7 I have *such / such a* big feet that I can never find nice shoes.

8 I love my big sister. She's *such a / such an* amazing person.

5 Read the sentences and answer the questions.

1 The green sneakers are such a bargain!

2 Those dresses have such pretty colors.

A When does *a/an* follow *such*?

B When doesn't *a/an* follow *such*?

6 Complete the sentences with *such* or *such a/an*.

I'm having ___such a___ good time on vacation!

1 They are _____ interesting people! I love talking to them.

2 Tom has done _____ silly thing. He's going to get into trouble!

3 Have you ever eaten _____ awful steak?

4 My brother always reads _____ good books!

5 My mom's _____ good cook that my friends love to come to dinner.

6 Why did you choose _____ expensive present? We don't have enough money.

7 Look at the places in the box. Write sentences using *such* or *such a/an*. Use the phrases below to help you. Then read your friend's sentences and guess the place.

> home   the park
> the movie theater
> the restaurant   downtown
> a concert hall   the beach

| funny movie | strange music |

| happy children | warm weather |

| awful pizza | noisy street |

I'm watching such a funny movie.

You're at the movie theater!

1 Read the brochure about the seasons in Yosemite National Park. When should people who love hiking visit the park?

Yosemite National Park is spectacular in all seasons!

Winter, spring, summer, or fall, the beauty of Yosemite National Park is always there for nature lovers!

Winter is the best time for you if you like snowboarding or skiing! If you don't have skiing equipment, you can rent it at one of our centers!

Spring is the perfect season if you like hiking or visiting the waterfalls!

Bring warm clothes and a good raincoat if you want to take long hikes in the mountains. The weather changes very quickly! If you come in April, rain and even snow are common.

Summer is the time to come if you want to see the whole park! All of the roads are open. If you don't want to wait in a long line, you have to be at the park entrance before mid-morning.

In summer, it doesn't rain much, so some of the waterfalls are almost dry. It's the right time to visit if you like wild flowers.

If there is something tourists love in **fall**, it is the color of Yosemite Park's trees. Their colors are at their best if the weather is cool and dry, but the temperatures don't go below 0°C.

2 Read and complete with one or two words.

People who like skiing should visit Yosemite National Park in .... *winter* ....

1 You can .... skiing equipment there if you don't have any.

2 In Yosemite, it may rain or snow ....

3 If you like wild flowers, visit Yosemite in ....

4 At Yosemite, it .... very little in summer.

5 The trees' colors are best when .... is cool.

3 Read the brochure again. Underline three sentences with _if_. Then fill in the table.

4 Circle the correct answer.

1 If you heat ice, it _is melting / melts_.

2 The river _freezes / is freezing_ if it's very cold.

3 I _walk / walks_ to school if the weather is nice.

4 If people _don't / doesn't_ eat well, they aren't healthy.

5 If babies are hungry, they _cries / cry_.

Grammar

Winter **is** the best time for you if you **like** snowboarding.

If you .... in April, rain and snow **are** common.

If you .... to wait in a long line, you **have** to come early.

5 Read the sentences. Do they have the same meaning? What tense is before and after _if_? Discuss with a friend.

1 Spring is the perfect time if you want to see the waterfalls in Yosemite.

2 If you want to see the waterfalls in Yosemite, spring is the perfect time.

6 Complete the sentences with the correct form of the verbs.

1 If it _____ (rain), I wear my rubber boots.

2 Plants die if you _____ (not/water) them.

3 If you freeze water, it _____ (become) ice.

4 If we _____ (play) loud music, the neighbors aren't happy.

5 If you _____ (not/sleep) well, you feel tired.

6 Dogs bite if they _____ (be) scared.

7 Complete the sentences about yourself.

I cook if my parents are at work.

1 If it rains, _____ .

2 I get sick if I _____ .

3 If I miss my grandpa, _____ .

4 I get grumpy if _____ .

5 I run if _____ .

8 Read the text about the Everglades National Park. Choose the best word (A, B, or C) for each space.

The Everglades National Park is in south Florida. *A* you want to visit the Everglades, you have to know that there are only **(1)** seasons: the summer wet season and the winter dry season. The winter dry season runs **(2)** November to March and the summer wet season runs from April to November.

Most people visit **(3)** Everglades in the winter dry season. If they come then, they **(4)** see the different types of birds that come to enjoy the warm winters. There aren't many tours in the summer wet season. So, if you **(5)** to visit the Everglades in the summer wet season, you have to check on the website **(6)** coming.

(7) are three different entrances to the Everglades. They are in three different cities and they are not connected. If you want to visit the Everglades, you **(8)** to take your car. There is no public transportation within **(9)** park and the distances are very long. The **(10)** popular visitor center is Ernest F. Coe Visitor Center. It is open all year.

	(A) If	B When	C It
1	A three	B two	C one
2	A to	B since	C from
3	A a	B the	C these
4	A cans	B can	C can't
5	A don't want	B wants	C want
6	A after	B before	C then
7	A There	B Those	C These
8	A has	B have	C are having
9	A a	B the	C some
10	A most	B more	C best

You promised to go swimming with me!

1 Read the dialog. When is Nadia going to do her homework?

Rocio:	Why aren't you ready? You promised to go swimming with me!
Nadia:	I know and I really want to go, but our teacher gave us a bunch of homework!
Rocio:	You can't have that much!
Nadia:	Yes, I do! I need to learn this list of French words by heart, do five math problems, and write an essay for tomorrow!
Rocio:	Are you sure it's all for tomorrow?
Nadia:	Of course! Look! Here's my notebook!
Rocio:	I think you should try not to read instructions too quickly. The math homework is for next week, and the French words are for Friday.
Nadia:	Are you sure?
Rocio:	Of course, here, look at your teacher's note.
Nadia:	Wow, that's great! Thanks, Rocio! Give me a minute. I'll get my things.
Nadia's mom:	Hi, Rocio! Where are you going, Nadia? I thought you had a lot of homework.
Nadia:	No, I don't, Mom. I just need to write a short essay. I'll do it when I come back from the swimming pool.
Nadia's mom:	OK, just don't forget to do it!

2 Read and answer the questions.

1 Did Nadia read her teacher's instructions correctly?

....

2 What's Nadia's homework for tomorrow? ....

3 Does Nadia want to go to the swimming pool? ....

4 When is Nadia's French homework due? ....

5 Does Rocio think Nadia has a lot of homework? ....

Grammar

Nadia **promised to go** to the swimming pool with Rocio.

Nadia **wants to go** swimming with Rocio.

She should **try not to read** instructions too quickly.

3 Read the dialog again. Underline verbs followed by _to_ + verb.

4 Circle the correct answer.

Joel: Hi, Dad! Did you *remember to* / *remember* buy my new computer game?

Dad: Yes, here it is! But I **(1)** *refuses to* / *refuse to* give it to you now. You have to **(2)** *promise to* / *promising* wait until after dinner to play with it.

Joel: Oh, Dad!

Dad: No game until you **(3)** *agree to* / *agree* have dinner first.

Joel: OK! It's a deal: I **(4)** *promise not to* / *not promise to* play before dinner.

Dad: And you **(5)** *need to cleaning* / *need to clean* up after dinner, too. It's your turn.

5 What's different? Where is *not* in the second sentence? Can you shorten it? Discuss with a friend.

1 Nadia should learn to plan her time carefully.

2 Nadia should try not to read instructions too quickly.

6 Put the words in order.

1 to want I German learn ....

2 Dad not promised to late be ....

3 glasses buy she to needs new ....

4 forgot I Grandma to on call birthday her

....

5 agreed my brother not I to with fight

....

6 my I homework do to remembered ....

7 Tell your friend some facts about yourself using the verbs in the box. He/She has to guess whether it's true or not.

begin forget learn agree need
promise remember start try want

I promised to eat my greens last night.

That's false. You don't like broccoli!

8 **Read the story. Write some words to complete the sentences about the story. You can use 1, 2, 3, or 4 words.**

Adam, Petra, and Jack always walk back from school along the river. One day, they heard a strange sound. "What's that?" said Jack.

"It's a little dog," said Adam.

"He's trying to swim to the bank!" said Petra. "He's almost there, but he's very tired."

"Let's make a rope with our belts and throw it to him," said Jack. "When he catches it, we can pull him out of the river."

The children made a rope with their belts. "Catch the rope!" they shouted. But the little dog was tired and scared. He barked but he did not catch the rope.

Finally, he bit the end of the rope and the children started to pull. Little by little, they pulled the small dog out of the river.

"What a pretty little dog!" said Petra. "I'd love to take you home, but we already have two dogs."

"We have a cat at home," said Jack. "What about you, Adam?"

"I've always wanted a pet. Do you want to come with me, little dog?" asked Adam. The little dog wagged his tail and walked toward Adam.

"Great! He agrees," said the children. They all started walking home, and the little dog followed Adam happily.

The three children always walked home by .... *the river* ....

One day they heard a strange .... *sound* ....

1 The little dog was trying .... to the bank.

2 The children made a rope with their ....

3 The little dog didn't catch the rope because he was ....

4 The children pulled the little dog out of the ....

5 Petra can't take the dog home because her family ....

6 Jack has .... at home.

7 The little dog was very happy to go home with ....

1 Read the dialog. Where will the family go for their vacation?

Dad: Have you all thought about our summer vacation? Where should we go?

Sally: We could go to an amusement park. We've never been to one!

Mom: If we go to an amusement park, you and your brother will fight over which one we choose.

Sally: I want to visit Water Kingdom. I love swimming!

Billy: No way! That's boring. I want to go to Animal World.

Sally: What's that?

Billy: You can take the jungle trails and see wild animals there. There are also some movie-themed rides. Mom, you'll love it!

Dad: What do you say, Connie? It sounds interesting.

Mom: Look! While you were talking, I looked up the website on the internet. Wow! The photos are amazing! It says we can hike among magical mountains. And there is a journey down a river to see a realistic rainforest!

Billy: Will you let me ride the fastest roller coaster if we go there, Mom?

Mom: If we go, Billy, you'll have to behave!

2 Read and complete with one or two words.

1 The family has .... been to an amusement park.

2 Sally wants to visit ....

3 If they go to an amusement park, Billy will ride .... roller coaster.

4 Mom has .... up the website on the internet.

5 The family are talking about their .... vacation.

3 Read the dialog again. Underline sentences with _if_.

Grammar

If we **visit** Pisa, we'**ll see** the Leaning Tower.

If we **go** to the movies, we **won't have** money for pizza.

Will you **help** me with Spanish if I **help** you with English?

4 Match to make sentences.

1 If I don't finish my homework,
2 If you are late to school again,
3 You will miss the bus
4 If the students don't have any homework,
5 I will travel to a theme park this summer
6 Dad won't drive us to school

A your teacher won't be happy.
B if I pass my exams.
C if we don't ask him.
D if you don't hurry up.
E I won't go to the movies.
F they will play frisbee in the park.

5 Read the sentences and answer the questions.

1 If you go to Japan, you'll eat ramen every day.
2 You'll eat ramen every day if you go to Japan.

A What is the tense in the first part of sentence one?
B What is the tense in the second part of sentence one?
C Does sentence two mean the same as sentence one?

6 Complete the sentences with the correct form of the verbs.

1 If you _____ (eat) an apple every day, you'll be very healthy.
2 You _____ (not/pass) your test if you don't study.
3 Will the children play in the yard if it _____ (not/rain)?
4 If you want to be an astronaut, you _____ (have to) study hard.
5 If I _____ (cook) some eggs, how many will you eat?

7 Complete the sentences about a friend. Ask your friend if you guessed correctly.

If you get good grades,... You'll feel good if... If your little brother... You'll feel bad if... If you get into trouble,...

You'll feel bad if you don't pass the test next week.

Yes! My turn. If your little brother touches your computer...

8 Look at the pictures. Write about this story. Write 20 or more words.

....

....

....

....

....

My dad told me to get good grades

1 Read the dialogs. Why must Enzo get good grades?

Mom: Caroline, go to the library and pick up a book for me, please.

Caroline: Sure, Mom.

Teacher: Enzo, your math grade is not good at all! Can't you pay more attention in class? And you mustn't be late for school again! Sorry, but I'll have to talk to your parents.

Caroline: Hi, Enzo! You look sad.

Enzo: Well, I had a conversation with Mr. Williamson, my teacher.

Caroline: What did he say?

Enzo: He asked me to pay more attention in class, and he told me not to be late for school again.

Caroline: Well, that's not too bad!

Enzo: Well, he also told me my math grade wasn't good. He's going to talk to my parents. My dad told me to get good grades. If I don't, I can't go on vacation. Anyway, where are you going?

Caroline: To the library. Mom asked me to pick up a book for her. Do you want to come?

Enzo: Sure!

Caroline: Hi, Mrs. Lyons. My mom asked me to pick up a book for her.

Librarian: Hi, Caroline! Here it is! Could she bring it back by May 20?

Caroline: Yes, of course. Thank you.

2 Read and circle T (*true*) or F (*false*).

1 Caroline's mom has to bring the book back by May 20.   T / F

2 Enzo's mom told him to get good grades.   T / F

3 Enzo is often late for class.   T / F

4 Enzo had a conversation with his dad.   T / F

5 Enzo's teacher asked him to pay more attention in class.   T / F

Grammar

My teacher **asked** me **to pay** more attention in class.

My mom **asked** me **to pick up** a book for her.

My dad **told** me **to get** good grades.

My teacher **told** me **not to be** late for school again.

3 Read the dialogs again. Underline sentences in reported speech.

4 Circle the correct answer.

1 Last night Dad asked Daiki *to mail / mail* a letter.

2 My mom told me *to forget not / not to forget* to buy butter.

3 Julio asked Damien *buy him / to buy him* a large envelope.

4 Dad told Leo *not to talk / to not talk* to strangers.

5 Grandma asked me *help her / to help her* with the cleaning.

5 Read the sentences. What elements change? What elements stay the same? Discuss with a friend.

1 "Pass me the salt, please," my brother asked. ➜ My brother asked me to pass him the salt.

2 "Don't be late," she told us. ➜ She told us not to be late.

3 "Can you help me?" he asked. ➜ He asked me to help him.

6 Imagine you have to tell your parents about a talk you had with a teacher. Write the sentences.

"Come in and sit down," the teacher told me. ➜ *The teacher told me to come in and sit down.*

1 "Don't close the door," she told me. ➜ She told me ....

2 "Sit still, please." she asked. ➜ She asked me ....

3 "Give me your test, please," she told me. ➜ She ....

4 "Don't forget to do your homework!" she told me. ➜

She ....

5 "Please, help me with the books," she asked. ➜

She ....

7 Think about last week. What did members of your family ask you to do? What did they tell you to do? Write.

My sister asked me to help her with her homework.

1 My mom asked me to ....

2 My dad told me ....

3 ....

4 ....

5 ....

8 **Read the email and write the missing words. Write one word on each line.**

Dear Berat,

My family and I discussed our plans _____*for*_____ our winter break last night. Guess what! We're **(1)** _____ to go skiing in Sweden! Mom was very happy. She loves skiing!

Dad **(2)** _____ me to get good grades. If I don't pass all my tests, I **(3)** _____ go with them. I'm kind of worried because I didn't do very well on my last English test. My teacher **(4)** _____ me to see her after class tomorrow. I hope she won't give me extra work!

What about you? What are **(5)** _____ plans for the winter break? Please, email back quickly!

Frank

1 **Read Michio's blog. What was his resolution?**

Sunday

Tomorrow I begin a new healthy life. Eating well and doing sports is simple, isn't it? I'll write about my progress on my blog every day before going to school.

Monday

From today until Friday, I will wake up at 6:30 a.m. and run for half an hour around the block.  At 7:30 a.m., I will have cornflakes and milk for breakfast. Mom will drive me to school at 8 a.m.

Tuesday

Today I woke up at 7 a.m. I'll just dress and have breakfast. This afternoon I have my first session at the gym, so I'll skip running.

Wednesday

Yesterday I went to the gym, so this morning I was too tired to run. I woke up late and Mom can't drive me to school, so I don't have time for breakfast. Walking to school counts as exercise, doesn't it? My brother thinks I'm cheating, but I think I'm doing OK.

Thursday

Today I have baseball practice at 4 p.m., so I don't have to run around the block, do I? I had pancakes for breakfast.

Friday

Today I had pancakes for breakfast again. 😣 I might start my health plan again next week!

2 **Read and answer the questions. Use no more than five words.**

1 When is Michio planning to write about his progress? ....

2 What time is he going to get up every day? ....

3 Did he get up at 6:30 a.m. on Tuesday? ....

4 Why didn't Michio have breakfast on Wednesday? ....

5 What might Michio do next week? ....

3 **Read Michio's blog again. Underline sentences with question tags.**

4 Match the sentences to the correct question tags.

1 A: We're having dinner at Lizzie's tonight,
2 B: I hope she isn't cooking! She isn't a very good cook,
3 A: Oh! It'll be all right! Her husband is cooking. He's an excellent cook,
4 B: You're sure about this,
5 A: Of course I am! I have dinner with them every Friday,
6 B: OK, then. Tom and Ellen are also coming. They're bringing the dessert,

A don't I?
B aren't they?
C is she?
D aren't you?
E isn't he?
F aren't we?

5 Complete the dialog with the correct form of the verbs.

C: When _does_ your aunt _arrive_ (arrive) from Canberra?
D: Her plane **(1)** _____ (arrive) tomorrow at 9:45 p.m.
C: What time **(2)** _____ the movie _____ (start) on Friday?
D: Charlie says it **(3)** _____ (start) at 4 p.m.
C: No! It **(4)** _____ (end) at 4 p.m. It **(5)** _____ (begin) at 2:15 p.m.

6 Complete using *such* or *such a/an*.

1 I'm sure Tom will pass his exams. He's _____ hardworking boy.
2 I've never eaten _____ awful pizza. We'll never come here again!
3 She always wears _____ elegant clothes!
4 Thanks for driving me home! You're _____ good friend.
5 They're _____ interesting people!
6 I didn't know she lived in _____ nice house.

7 Think of two true and two false facts about yourself. Use the words in the box to help you. Your friend guesses which sentences are true and which are false.

begin forget learn love need promise remember start try want

I promised to stop playing computer games.

That's false! You love computer games.

8 Read the article about the origins of writing. Choose the best word (A, B, or C) for each space.

Imagine you are a prehistoric man __B__ is living in a dull cave 35,000 years ago. You **(1)** .... decorate the walls with paintings of your hands. But suppose that your cave is near a place **(2)** .... hunting is good. **(3)** .... you want to point this out to your friends, you could draw some animals on the walls of your cave. This is how written communication started.

Little by little, people moved from drawings on the walls of caves to writing on tablets made **(4)** .... clay. By 2000 B.C., people **(5)** .... send letters written on clay tablets to members of their family who lived in faraway places. But these tablets broke **(6)** ....

Between 500 B.C. and 170 B.C., the Egyptians used a plant to make a flexible writing surface. This was better than the clay tablets. Then, in the year 105 B.C., Cai Lun, a Chinese man, **(7)** .... wood to make paper for the first time. Paper came to Europe in A.D.1056. Until this time, people wrote on sheets **(8)** .... of cow skin.

	A which	(B) who	C where
1	A will	B could	C shall
2	A that	B where	C when
3	A What	B But	C If
4	A of	B out	C at
5	A can	B will	C could
6	A happily	B easy	C easily
7	A made	B used	C use
8	A make	B makes	C made

1 Read the article. Which of the two animals is larger?

They haven't changed in thousands of years!

Home **Nature** Science Technology

If you think that direct descendants from prehistoric animals don't exist, you'll be surprised!

This is a Komodo dragon. It lives on the Komodo Islands, in Indonesia, and it is the largest meat-eating lizard in the world. Komodo dragons haven't changed since the Komodo Islands separated from Australia, 900,000 years ago. They have lived on the islands for millions of years.

Scientists have found fossils of Komodo dragons that are 3.8 million years old.

A Komodo dragon can grow to be 3 meters long and weigh 130 kg. Komodo dragons are protected animals. There are only about 5,000 of them left in the world.

The tuatara is a reptile that lives in New Zealand. It's the only descendant of animals that lived 200 million years ago. The tuatara are greenish brown, they can be up to 80 cm long, and they have a crest along their back. They can live to be 100 years old. If a tuatara loses its tail, it grows back. They also have a "third eye", which you can only see in baby tuataras. Scientists still don't know what they use it for.

2 Read and answer the questions.

1 How old are the fossils of Komodo dragons? ....

2 How many Komodo dragons are left in the world? ....

3 Where do tuatara live? ....

4 How long can the tuatara live? ....

5 What is the tuatara's third eye for? ....

3 Read the text again. Underline sentences in Present Perfect in blue and conditional sentences in red.

4 Circle the correct answer.

A Silly Bank Robber

A man **(1)** *walked / was walked* into a bank. When he was inside, he took a sheet of the bank's notepaper and **(2)** *wrote / was writing* a note for the teller. The note said, "Put all the money in the bag." Then he stood in line.

While he **(3)** *was waiting / was waited*, he thought, "Somebody may have seen me write the note." So, he **(4)** *went / was going* to the bank across the street and waited in line there. When the bank teller read his note, she **(5)** *was saying / said*, "This note is for a teller at the bank across the street."

The bank robber said, "I'm sorry!" He crossed the street and went into the first bank again. While he **(6)** *crossed / was crossing* the street, the teller called the police. When the robber arrived at the bank, the police **(7)** *waited / were waiting* for him!

5 Complete the text with the correct form of the verbs. Use Present Perfect or Past Simple.

Angkor, in Cambodia, is one of the most important archeological centers in the world. It _____*was*_____ (be) the capital of the Khmer Kingdom from the ninth to fifteenth centuries. For years, archeologists **(1)** _____ (try) to find out why people **(2)** _____ (leave) it in A.D.1434. But nobody **(3)** _____ (find) the reason yet.

Many tourists **(4)** _____ (visit/already) Angkor and many more will visit. This **(5)** _____ (help/already) to bring a lot of money to restore the buildings. Thanks to this, restoration works **(6)** _____ (not stop) since 1992.

6 Complete the sentences with the correct form of the verbs.

What _____*do*_____ *you* _____*need*_____ *(need) if you* _____*want*_____ *(want) to send a letter?*

1   If I _____ (see) my grandmother, I _____ (ask) her for the recipe.

2   If you _____ (go) out without a jacket, you _____ (get) sick.

3   If you _____ (heat) ice, it _____ (melt).

4   I'm allergic to peanuts. If I _____ (eat) them, I _____ (feel) bad.

5   If you _____ (not/study) hard, you _____ (not/get) good grades on the final test.

7 Choose four of these people and think of something they told you. Then tell a friend what he or she said. Your friend has to guess who said it.

| your teacher | your mom | your dad | your grandpa |

| a police officer | a park ranger | your uncle | a friend | a zookeeper |

She told me not to be late.

Your mom!

No! My teacher. Your turn...

8 Read Nuray's blog and write the missing words. Write one word on each line.

Yesterday I went to the zoo ___with___ my family, and you won't believe what happened!

We went **(1)** _____ see the tropical birds, first. They **(2)** _____ beautiful! Mom and I loved them, but my brother Emre was bored, so we **(3)** _____ to see the monkeys.

The monkeys were definitely enjoying **(4)** _____. We were having fun looking at **(5)** _____, when we heard someone yell, "The lion **(6)** _____ escaped from its cage! Run!" People started running in all directions. We saw ten zookeepers run to the lion's cage. It was such **(7)** _____ scary moment!

Some time later, one **(8)** _____ the zookeepers came back and told us **(9)** _____ to worry. The lion was in its cage again. So, we **(10)** _____ continue our visit.

Irregular Verbs List

Infinitive	Past Simple	Past participle
be	was/were	been
become	became	become
begin	began	begun
bite	bit	bitten
break	broke	broken
bring	brought	brought
build	built	built
buy	bought	bought
catch	caught	caught
choose	chose	chosen
come	came	come
cost	cost	cost
cut	cut	cut
do	did	done
draw	drew	drawn
drink	drank	drunk
drive	drove	driven
eat	ate	eaten
fall	fell	fallen
feed	fed	fed
feel	felt	felt
fight	fought	fought
find	found	found
fly	flew	flown
forget	forgot	forgotten
get	got	gotten
give	gave	given
go	went	gone
grow	grew	grown
have	had	had
hear	heard	heard
hold	held	held
hurt	hurt	hurt
keep	kept	kept
know	knew	known
lay	laid	laid
lead	led	led

Infinitive	Past Simple	Past participle
leave	left	left
let	let	let
lie	lay	lain
lose	lost	lost
make	made	made
mean	meant	meant
meet	met	met
pay	paid	paid
put	put	put
read	read	read
ride	rode	ridden
ring	rang	rung
run	ran	run
say	said	said
see	saw	seen
sell	sold	sold
send	sent	sent
set	set	set
shake	shook	shaken
sing	sang	sung
sit	sat	sat
sleep	slept	slept
speak	spoke	spoken
spend	spent	spent
spread	spread	spread
stand	stood	stood
take	took	taken
teach	taught	taught
tell	told	told
think	thought	thought
throw	threw	thrown
understand	understood	understood
wake	woke	woken
wear	wore	worn
win	won	won
write	wrote	written

Pearson Education Limited

KAO Two
KAO Park
Harlow
Essex
CM17 9NA
England
and Associated Companies throughout the world.

www.English.com

First published 2019
Ninth impression 2022
ISBN: 978-1-292-21969-1

Set in Daytona Pro Primary 12/16pt

Printed and bound by CPI Group (UK) Ltd, Croydon CR0 4YY

Acknowledgements

The review sections were written by Chris Speck.

The publisher would like to thank the following for their kind permission to reproduce their photographs:

(Key: b-bottom; c-centre; l-left; r-right; t-top)

123RF.com: 21tr, 21br, 32/1, 37b, 42bl, 59t, 59b, Anatoly Fedotov 32/7, angellodeco 29, dimarik16 56c, Idanbury 12r, ivanmateev 33br, macsim 4r, saiko3p 21bl; **Pearson Education Ltd:** Studio 8 49, Jon Barlow 6, 9, 36l, Gareth Boden 21tl, 52tl, 52tr, 52b, Pearson Education, Inc. 16, Arvind Singh Negi / Red Reef Design Studio. Pearson India Education Services Pvt. Ltd 23, Jules Selmes 32/2, Sozaijiten 41/3; **Shutterstock.com:** 1107155 26, Africa Studio 32/3, 33bl, Alexandr Makarov 32/8, Andresr 35t, Andy Z 44tl, anyaivanova 19, auremar 4l, Barbara A. Harvey 27, Barbro Bergfeldt 39b, ChameleonsEye 53b, Chepurnova Oxana 32/5, Colin D. Young 44tr, CREATISTA 33t, 35b, Daniel Taeger 53tl, Darren Baker 41/5, Digital Media Pro 55, Dustie 46, ejwhite 47, Ferenc Szelepcsenyi 42t, Firma V 10l, Fotokostic 36r, Galyna Andrushko 44bl, holbox 22l, ilolab 39t, iofoto 56t, Ivonne Wierink 33c, Jordan Tan 14, kongsak sumano 13, KPG_Payless 56b, Lana B 61, Lisa F. Young 48, 53tr, LuckyPhoto 42br, Maksim Dubinsky 37t, Marcio Jose Bastos Silva 58, Mike Flippo 33bc, Miks 31, Monkey Business Images 10r, 34, 35c, 50, monticello 32/6, nito 15, Paul Cotney 8, prochasson frederic 22r, Richard Susanto 44br, Sergiy Zavgorodny 17, siamionau pavel 43, sonya etchison 7b, Stephen Coburn 41/4, stockyimages 41/2, Taras Vyshnya 12l, wavebreakmedia 7t, 41/1, yamix 32/4

All other images © Pearson Education

Cover photo © **Getty Images:** Kerkez

Illustrated by

Matt Ward (Beehive Illustration) 16.

Unknown reuse artists: 23